WRITTEN BY JANICE WEAVER • ILLUSTRATED BY BONNIE SHEMIE

BUILDING AMERICA

TUNDRA BOOKS

Text copyright © 2002 by Janice Weaver

Illustrations copyright © 2002 by Bonnie Shemie

Published in Canada by Tundra Books,
481 University Avenue, Toronto, Ontario M5G 2E9

Published in the United States by Tundra Books of Northern New York,
P.O. Box 1030, Plattsburgh, New York 12901

Library of Congress Control Number: 2002101146

National Library of Canada Cataloguing in Publication Data

Weaver, Janice

    Building America

Includes index.

ISBN 0-88776-606-4

1. Architecture—United States—History. I. Shemie, Bonnie, 1949- II. Title.

NA705.W42 2002   720'.973   C2002-900782-8

We acknowledge the support of the Canada Council for the Arts and the Ontario Arts Council for our
publishing program.

We acknowledge the financial support of the Government of Canada through the Book Publishing
Industry Development Program for our publishing activities.

Design: Blaine Herrmann

Medium: watercolour on paper

Printed in Hong Kong, China

1 2 3 4 5 6   07 06 05 04 03 02

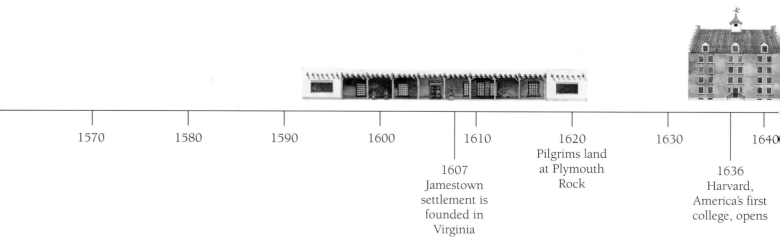

1570   1580   1590   1600   1610   1620   1630   1640

1607
Jamestown
settlement is
founded in
Virginia

1620
Pilgrims land
at Plymouth
Rock

1636
Harvard,
America's first
college, opens

For my parents, who made this book – and everything else – possible
– J.W.

For May Cutler
– B.S.

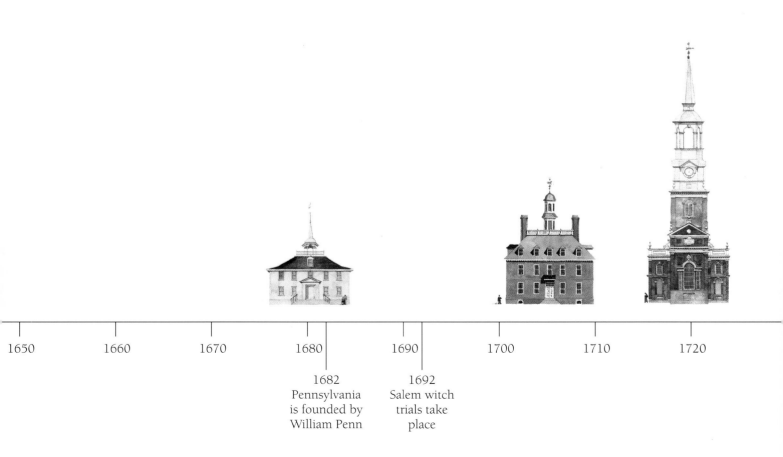

1650	1660	1670	1680	1690	1700	1710	1720

1682
Pennsylvania
is founded by
William Penn

1692
Salem witch
trials take
place

ACKNOWLEDGEMENTS

This book came together with the help of the following people and organizations: the McGill, Westmount, and Toronto Reference libraries; the Library of Congress, whose Historic American Buildings Survey Web site provided many useful photographs and drawings, and much important background material; Mark Gerlenter, whose *History of American Architecture* is a useful overview that also introduced us to Henry Trost's wonderful Second Owls Club in Tucson, Arizona; Alison Reid, who proved that even editors need editing; Leland Roth, the dean of American architectural history; Bruce R. Schulman, whose Web site for the 1893 World's Columbian Exposition is both informative and entertaining; and most of all, our respective families: Milo, Khuther (Bill), Ben, and Daniel Shemie, and Robert and Audrey Weaver, David Weaver, and Mark Bell.

Thanks must also be given to our ever-enthusiastic publisher, Kathy Lowinger, and her excellent colleagues at Tundra Books: Cathy Francis, Catherine Mitchell, Alison Morgan, Kong Njo, Ariadne Patsiopoulos, and Sue Tate.

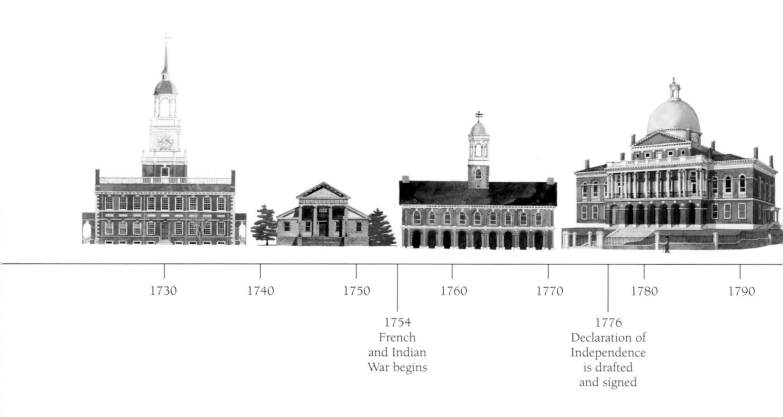

1730   1740   1750   1760   1770   1780   1790

1754
French
and Indian
War begins

1776
Declaration of
Independence
is drafted
and signed

CONTENTS

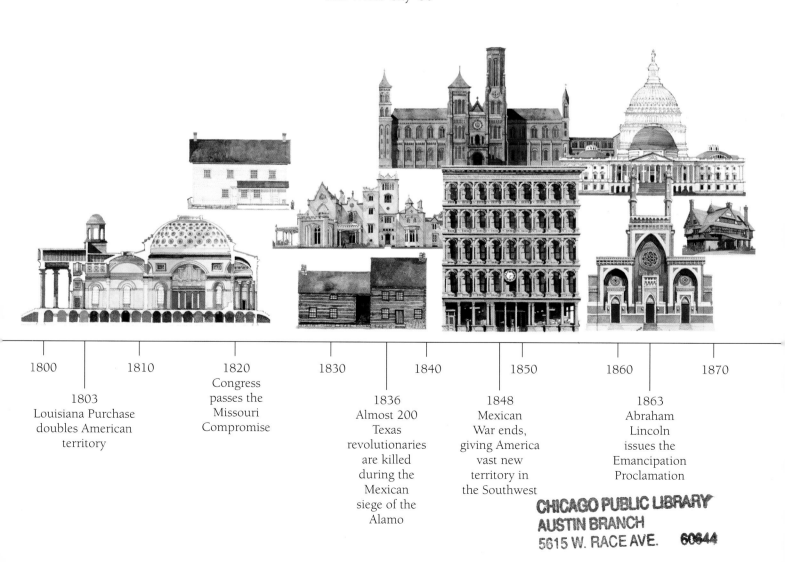

1800　　1810　　1820　　1830　　1840　　1850　　1860　　1870

1803
Louisiana Purchase
doubles American
territory

1820
Congress
passes the
Missouri
Compromise

1836
Almost 200
Texas
revolutionaries
are killed
during the
Mexican
siege of the
Alamo

1848
Mexican
War ends,
giving America
vast new
territory in
the Southwest

1863
Abraham
Lincoln
issues the
Emancipation
Proclamation

1880

1890
200 Sioux are
massacred by
government
troops at
Wounded
Knee, South
Dakota

1900

1901
President
William
McKinley is
assassinated

1910

1914
First
World
War
begins

1920

1930

1929
Stock
market
crashes

1940

1939
Second
World
War
begins

INTRODUCTION

The landscape of America is more than just lakes and rivers, canyons and deserts; it's also the buildings that surround us – the soaring skyscrapers, monumental cathedrals, neighborhood schoolhouses, and grand private homes. These buildings are so much more than somewhere to go to work, pray, or be educated. Through the form they take, the materials they're made of, even the sites they sit on, most buildings say a lot about who we are and what we believe in.

This book travels through almost 400 years of history and to all four corners of the continental United States to explore an architecture that is as diverse as the people who created it. From old favorites like Monticello and the Chrysler Building to lesser-known treasures like Bernard Maybeck's First Church of Christ, Scientist, the buildings we'll visit tell the story of a nation and its people.

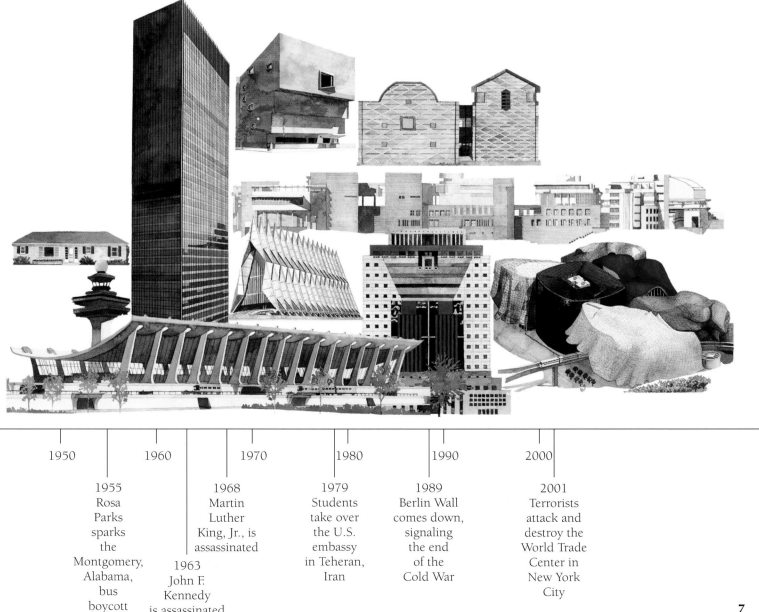

1950   1960   1970   1980   1990   2000

1955
Rosa
Parks
sparks
the
Montgomery,
Alabama,
bus
boycott

1963
John F.
Kennedy
is assassinated

1968
Martin
Luther
King, Jr., is
assassinated

1979
Students
take over
the U.S.
embassy
in Teheran,
Iran

1989
Berlin Wall
comes down,
signaling
the end
of the
Cold War

2001
Terrorists
attack and
destroy the
World Trade
Center in
New York
City

FIRST SETTLERS

In 1513, the Spaniard Juan Ponce de Léon set sail for Florida in search of the Fountain of Youth, that mythical spring that was supposed to make the old young again. Ponce de Léon was only one in a long line of adventurers and ordinary people who came to the New World on quests of one kind or another – for immortality, for gold and other riches, for religious freedom, for a new life. But it all started with the Spanish, who in 1565 were the first Europeans to settle permanently in what we now know as the United States, establishing a fort at St. Augustine, in Florida. Before long, they were joined in their adventures by the French, who explored the fur-trading routes of the Mississippi River as far south as the Gulf of Mexico, and by the Dutch and English on the East Coast.

All of these settlers brought with them the building traditions of their former homes, and they were soon re-creating the look and feel of the places they'd left behind. Of course, America could be an unforgiving place, bone-chillingly cold in some areas and blistering hot in others, and the colonizers were often forced to build quickly and with whatever materials were at hand.

The Spanish were the only Europeans to acknowledge the usefulness of the building techniques of those who were here first. They combined their traditional construction methods with some they learned from the Native Americans they met as they explored the southern portion of the continent. The Dutch, by contrast, favored the techniques and even the materials of their native Holland for their short-lived colony of New Amsterdam (now New York City).

But the English proved to be the most successful settlers of all. By 1700, they had ten times as many colonists as France and many thousands of times more than Spain. They dominated the architecture of the New World too, filling the horizon with buildings that drew their inspiration from the island nation they'd left behind.

▼ Well-to-do Virginians often built solid homes that suggested the manor houses of England. Although its design is fairly simple, the brick **Adam Thoroughgood House** (Norfolk, Virginia, about 1690) has a substantiality that the homes of most early settlers lacked.

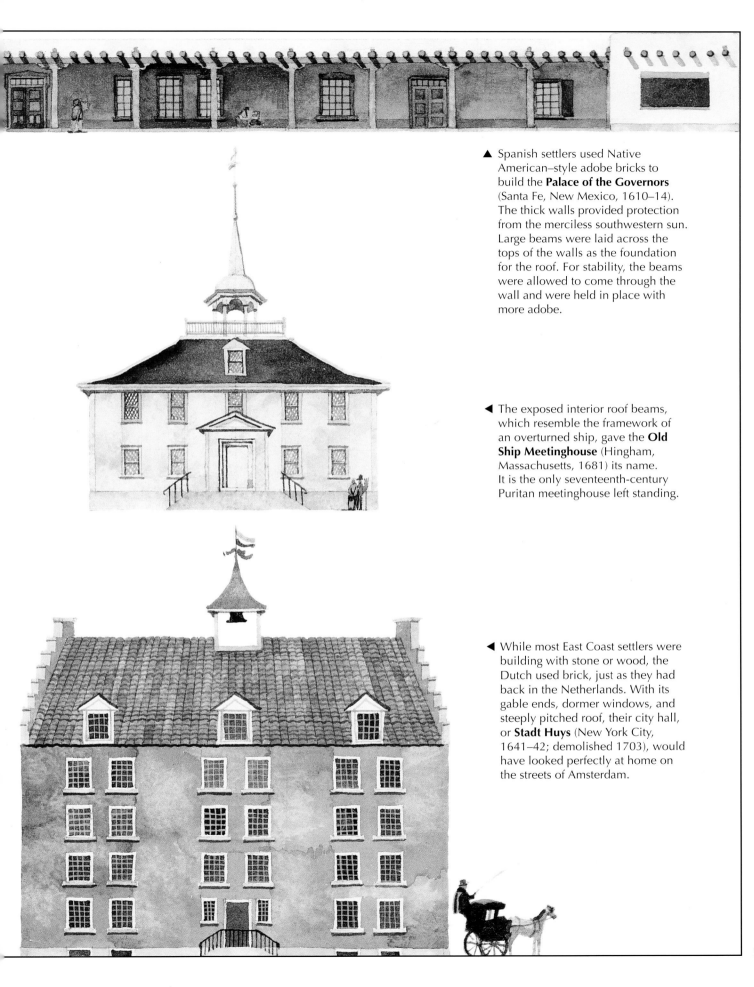

▲ Spanish settlers used Native American–style adobe bricks to build the **Palace of the Governors** (Santa Fe, New Mexico, 1610–14). The thick walls provided protection from the merciless southwestern sun. Large beams were laid across the tops of the walls as the foundation for the roof. For stability, the beams were allowed to come through the wall and were held in place with more adobe.

◄ The exposed interior roof beams, which resemble the framework of an overturned ship, gave the **Old Ship Meetinghouse** (Hingham, Massachusetts, 1681) its name. It is the only seventeenth-century Puritan meetinghouse left standing.

◄ While most East Coast settlers were building with stone or wood, the Dutch used brick, just as they had back in the Netherlands. With its gable ends, dormer windows, and steeply pitched roof, their city hall, or **Stadt Huys** (New York City, 1641–42; demolished 1703), would have looked perfectly at home on the streets of Amsterdam.

9

After 1700, the fledgling colonies really began to take hold and prosper. Immigrants were arriving by the thousands, eager to start over in this new land of promise. In just fifty years, from 1650 to 1700, the population of the thirteen British colonies jumped from 50,000 to more than 250,000. By the time another fifty years had passed, there would be more than two million people living in what had been a mere outpost for the great European powers not long before.

The American colonies were becoming a populous, thriving nation in their own right. And among the thousands who came were many skilled artisans, craftsmen, and builders, bringing with them a more sophisticated, mature form of architecture. Although they still most often built with wood, these new arrivals began disguising it to look like stone and ornamenting their buildings with details such as pediments, columns, and temple fronts that called to mind the ancient societies of Greece and Rome. No longer slapdash or temporary, these solid and elaborate buildings had a permanence that said America was here to stay.

Of course, all these newcomers needed someplace to live, and large cities soon began to emerge. Philadelphia, chartered in 1701, was perhaps the most important city in colonial America, and it was the first to be laid out on a grid pattern. The geometric plan, conceived by William Penn, the founder of Pennsylvania, was meant to block the spread of fire and disease, which had always been able to thrive in the tightly packed and haphazard streets of the major cities of Europe, such as London and Paris. To this day, the grid street plan is typical of North American cities.

Unfortunately, this period of peace, stability, and prosperity was not to last. By the time the century reached its midpoint, relations between the Thirteen Colonies and their mother country, England, had deteriorated beyond repair. War was on the horizon.

◀ Philadelphia's **Independence Hall** (Philadelphia, 1731–48), originally called the Old State House, is one of the best-known colonial buildings in America. The site of the signing of the Declaration of Independence, it marries the Baroque house form with a church-like tower, or steeple.

▶ Peter Harrison, the designer of the **Redwood Library** (Newport, Rhode Island, 1748–50), was what is known as a gentleman architect: he rarely accepted payment for his work. Because of its prominent portico, his neoclassical library looks very much like an ancient temple. He even scored and painted the wood walls to make them look like masonry (stone) blocks.

▶ With its symmetrical design, flat-topped roof, and decorative cupola, the **Governor's Palace** (Williamsburg, Virginia, 1706–20), like Independence Hall, was clearly inspired by Baroque houses in England. It was destroyed in 1781 but rebuilt in 1932, as part of the restoration of the entire colonial capital.

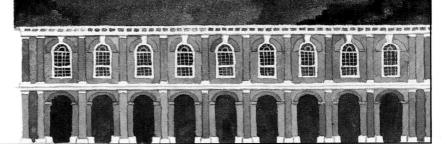

▶ **Faneuil Hall** (Boston, 1762), one of Boston's most loved landmarks, has been through many incarnations. The hall had to be rebuilt after a fire consumed the original 1742 structure, and it was then substantially expanded in 1805 by the influential architect Charles Bulfinch. Although Bulfinch doubled its size, he still left the 1762 structure almost intact. All that remains from the 1742 building, however, is the grasshopper weathervane that tops the decorative cupola.

THE AGE OF REVOLUTION

On the night of December 16, 1773, a group of colonists disguised as Native Americans boarded three ships anchored in Boston and unloaded their cargo of tea – right into the middle of the harbor. This was the Boston Tea Party, a protest of the British Parliament's authority over the Thirteen Colonies, and it set the colonists on the path to war with the mother country. America wouldn't know peace again until 1783.

When the revolutionary dust had settled, the colonists had a draft constitution (the Articles of Confederation), their own flag, and most important, their independence. A new nation had been born. Thomas Jefferson, the future president and a self-taught amateur architect, led the push to rid America of the influence of British architectural styles, just as the colonists had rid it of British rule. He believed he and his fellow Americans were creating a nation in the tradition of the great civilizations of Greece and Rome, and he wanted the architecture to reflect that. Buildings became a way to display, through bricks and mortar, the democratic ideals of those ancient societies, which had found new life in America.

Domes, temple fronts, columns, and other neoclassical details began to spring up on structures all over the young country. They could be found on private homes, like Jefferson's own Monticello; on government buildings, like Charles Bulfinch's Massachusetts State House; and on businesses, like Benjamin Henry Latrobe's Bank of Pennsylvania.

▼ Apart from the White House and George Washington's Mount Vernon, **Monticello** (Charlottesville, Virginia, 1796–1809) is probably the most famous home in America. Its unusual redesign (a more traditional house was built there between 1771 and 1782) shows that Thomas Jefferson had achieved some maturity as an architect. The building is a unique mix of neoclassical details that have their roots in both Greece and Rome.

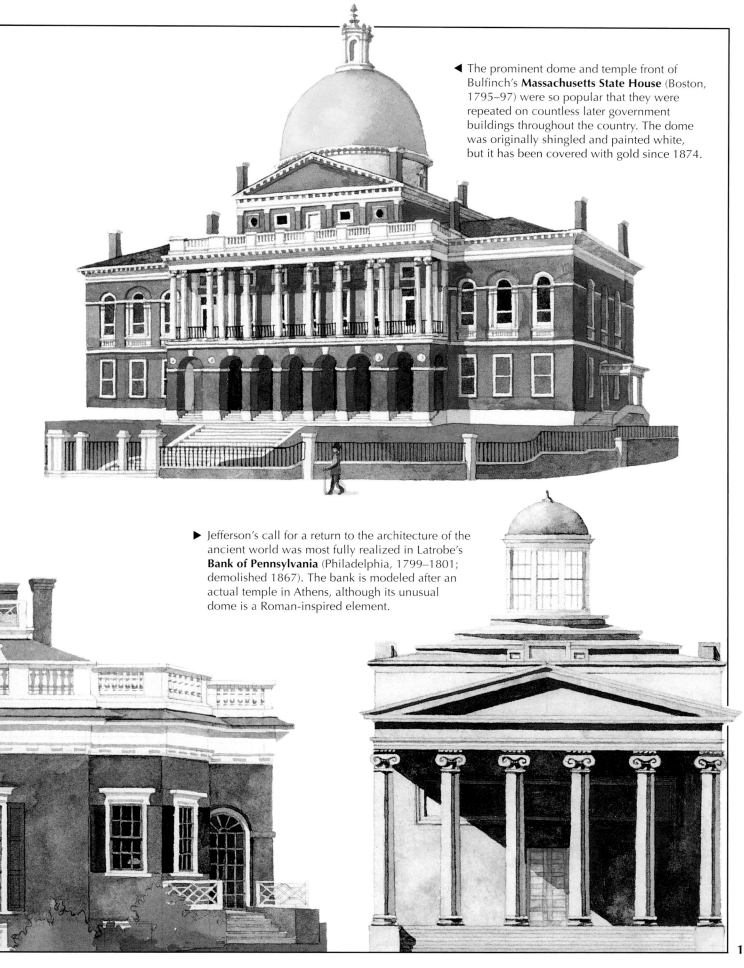

◀ The prominent dome and temple front of Bulfinch's **Massachusetts State House** (Boston, 1795–97) were so popular that they were repeated on countless later government buildings throughout the country. The dome was originally shingled and painted white, but it has been covered with gold since 1874.

▶ Jefferson's call for a return to the architecture of the ancient world was most fully realized in Latrobe's **Bank of Pennsylvania** (Philadelphia, 1799–1801; demolished 1867). The bank is modeled after an actual temple in Athens, although its unusual dome is a Roman-inspired element.

REVIVING THE OLD

America wasn't the only country undergoing massive changes. Soon after its revolution ended, one started in France. The Spanish empire, once so powerful and far-reaching, slipped into a steady decline. And England initiated what was possibly the most important transformation of them all, the Industrial Revolution.

The whole world was being shaken up and rearranged, and in America, the nation's leaders were soon looking beyond Greece and Rome for new ideas on how to model their society. The French Revolution inspired a renewed emphasis on liberty and equality, concepts that are fundamental in the United States to this day. Italy, Germany, and even England also provided political and cultural examples for those in the New World to follow.

Before long, America's architects were turning to these new sources of inspiration as well. The columns and pediments of the first half of the nineteenth century were left behind, and other architectural styles took their place. From England came the Gothic, a revival of a medieval building form characterized by asymmetry (irregularity) and a lot of ornamentation. Germany was the source of the Romanesque revival, which involved building on a grand scale, with textured surfaces, towers, and molded carvings. And Italy gave America its Renaissance revival, a lighter and more balanced type of architecture characterized by symmetrical windows, rounded arches, and a more graceful use of detailing.

These three styles, and many others, began to dramatically reshape the landscape of America – and their influence can still be seen today.

▼ It seems hard to believe today, but the Romanesque revival was a simpler, stripped-down version of the Gothic. Buildings like James Renwick's **Smithsonian Institution** (Washington, D.C., 1847–55) look heavily ornamented, but they were still less elaborate than many of their Gothic cousins. They were also cheaper and easier to build, which made them popular with architects, and they suited the skill level of the often less experienced American masons (stoneworkers).

▲ **Lyndhurst** (Tarrytown, New York, 1838–42), designed by Alexander Jackson Davis, is one of the finest Gothic revival houses in America. With its many projections and recesses, the castle-like building moves in and out, along both its height and its width, almost seeming to reach out to the land that surrounds it.

▶ John P. Gaynor used a newly developed material, cast iron, to build the **Haughwout** department store (New York City, 1857). The repetition and symmetry of the Renaissance revival style allowed Gaynor to create one mold for the window bays and use it again and again. The store looks like stone, but it was built without the expense of masons shaping it by hand. This was also the first public building to have a passenger elevator.

◀ When Richard Morris Hunt designed the **Tribune Building** (New York City, about 1872; demolished 1966), architects began to realize they could build up, instead of out. Although the first true skyscraper wouldn't be constructed for another eleven years, Hunt clearly already saw the value in providing a lot of office space on a relatively small piece of land.

▶ With its large Doric columns and second-floor *galerie* (porch), **Shadows-on-the-Teche** (New Iberia, Louisiana, 1831–34) combines elements of Greek and French design into the familiar plantation-style home. Unfortunately, houses like this seemed to have lost their place in America by the time the Civil War was over.

▼ Although it's really a Queen Anne design, H. H. Richardson's **W. Watts Sherman House** (Newport, Rhode Island, 1874–75) is often called the first Shingle Style house. Its tall chimney stacks, steep roofs, and lack of symmetry are all hallmarks of the later style.

▶ Built for a Southern cotton dealer, the **Isaac Bell House** (Newport, 1881–83) is typical of the large summer "cottages" that wealthy Americans built all over the oceanfront towns of the North. Covered entirely in shingles, it also shows a new influence – Japanese design – with exterior posts carved to look like bamboo and interior screens used in place of walls.

THE AGE OF COMMERCE

The middle of the nineteenth century was a time of great expansion – and great turmoil. The Mexican War, which ignited over land disputes in 1846, gave the United States control of Texas, California, Arizona, New Mexico, Nevada, Utah, and part of Colorado. But the admission of each new state increased tensions between the North and the South.

In 1860, South Carolina decided to secede (separate), and it was soon followed by ten more states, which together became known as the Confederacy. Within months, these states were involved in a terrible war, the Civil War, with the states of the North (the Union).

A lot of the tension between the North and the South was the result of differences in their economies. The South was a region still dependent on plantation farming and slavery, while the North was becoming wealthier and more industrialized. And once the war had been resolved – at the cost of 600,000 lives – and slavery had been stamped out, the inequalities only got worse. The South was a land destroyed, and the old social and economic systems were no more. But the North entered a period characterized by great energy and the free display of wealth.

While Southern farmers struggled to adapt to a life without slave labor, Northern merchants were building themselves elegant summer homes in well-to-do towns like Newport, Rhode Island. These buildings were proof that the nation's architecture was coming into its own. Soon America had its own unique type of architecture, called Shingle Style; several well-known architects, including Henry Hobson Richardson and Stanford White; and the first of the many tall towers that would eventually dominate the skylines of all its major cities.

HALLS OF POWER

Each country has buildings that symbolize the ideals it stands for. These are that country's most substantial structures, and they are built from the best materials by the most talented craftspeople. Traditionally, these buildings were either religious structures or places of royalty. The pyramids in Egypt, for example, were burial chambers for the pharaohs. The Parthenon in Athens was a temple for Athena, the Greek goddess of war and protector of cities. All over Western Europe, the grandest buildings were cathedrals (like Notre Dame in Paris) or royal palaces (like London's Buckingham Palace).

But in America, the most monumental structures were more likely to be public buildings. This is no surprise in a country that was founded not on a single religion or by followers of a king but on a form of government – democracy. Buildings like Charles Bulfinch's Massachusetts State House (see page 13) began to pay tribute to Greece and Rome, the ancient societies that invented democracy, as soon as the American Revolution had ended. Pediments, columns, domes, and porticos were all the rage for town halls, state houses, and other public buildings all over the nation. And although architects eventually turned to different countries and cultures for inspiration for other types of buildings, the neoclassical style continued to be used for government structures well into the twentieth century.

▼ Although George Washington laid the cornerstone in 1793, the **United States Capitol** wouldn't take the form we now know for almost three-quarters of a century. When it was burned by the British during the War of 1812, it was still incomplete, and both Benjamin Henry Latrobe and Charles Bulfinch had a hand in restoring it. But it was Thomas Ustick Walter's redesign (1851–65) that added the large wings on either side and the massive cast-iron dome that has become such a symbol of America.

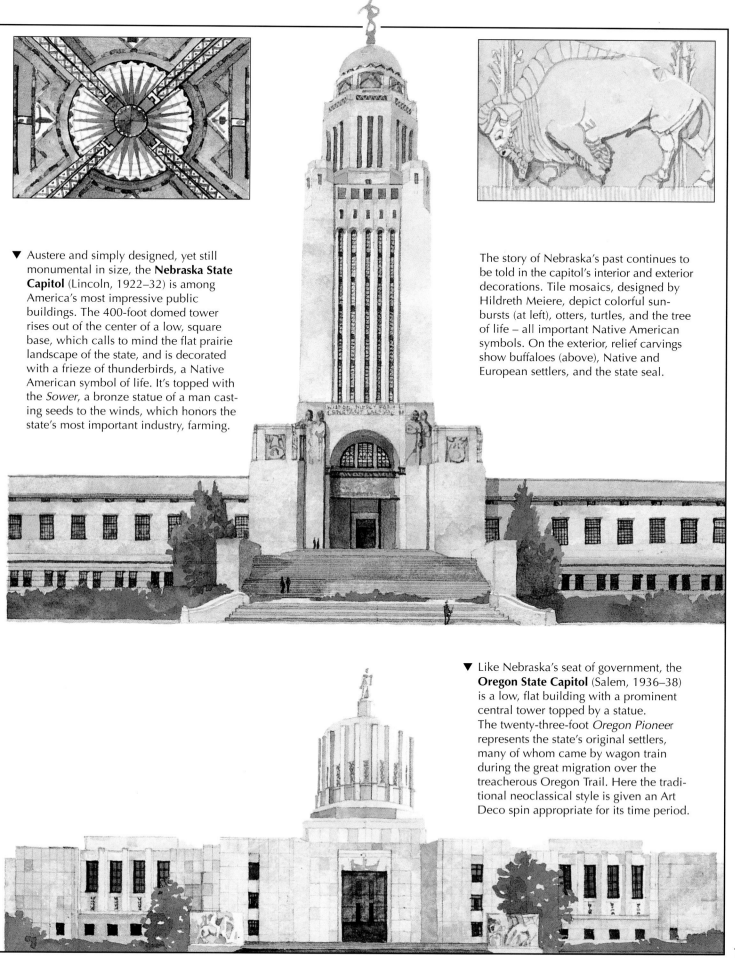

Austere and simply designed, yet still monumental in size, the **Nebraska State Capitol** (Lincoln, 1922–32) is among America's most impressive public buildings. The 400-foot domed tower rises out of the center of a low, square base, which calls to mind the flat prairie landscape of the state, and is decorated with a frieze of thunderbirds, a Native American symbol of life. It's topped with the *Sower*, a bronze statue of a man casting seeds to the winds, which honors the state's most important industry, farming.

The story of Nebraska's past continues to be told in the capitol's interior and exterior decorations. Tile mosaics, designed by Hildreth Meiere, depict colorful sunbursts (at left), otters, turtles, and the tree of life – all important Native American symbols. On the exterior, relief carvings show buffaloes (above), Native and European settlers, and the state seal.

Like Nebraska's seat of government, the **Oregon State Capitol** (Salem, 1936–38) is a low, flat building with a prominent central tower topped by a statue. The twenty-three-foot *Oregon Pioneer* represents the state's original settlers, many of whom came by wagon train during the great migration over the treacherous Oregon Trail. Here the traditional neoclassical style is given an Art Deco spin appropriate for its time period.

◄ The simplicity of the **Quaker meetinghouse** stands in stark contrast to the elaborate ornamentation of most other religious buildings. Because Quakerism is a religion with very little ritual attached to it, these meetinghouses were austere and had no pulpits or altars. Most had two sets of doors on the front; women and girls would enter through one, and boys and men through the other. Seating was usually plain wooden benches.

▼ Like most of the eighteenth-century California missions, **San Carlos de Borromeo** (Carmel, California, 1793–97) has a distinctly Spanish flavor, although it is made of locally quarried sandstone, not adobe. The walls lean in as they rise, and they finish off in a graceful arch, not a flat ceiling. This mission was established by a Franciscan monk, who came to what was at the time part of Mexico to convert the Native Americans to Catholicism.

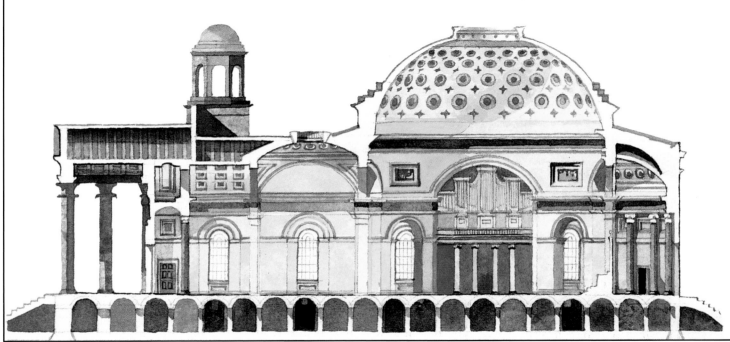

HOUSES OF WORSHIP

After two dangerous months at sea and a month spent exploring the coast around Cape Cod, the *Mayflower* finally landed at Plymouth Rock, in Massachusetts, on December 26, 1620. On board were 102 English Pilgrims, many of whom were followers of a stricter, more disciplined form of religious worship than was being offered by the Anglican Church. Called Puritans, these people wanted to escape the harassment and persecution they often suffered in England.

From the time the first Puritan set foot on that piece of Massachusetts soil, America has stood for religious tolerance and diversity. And the Puritans are not the only ones who came. The Shakers arrived in the late 1700s, and Jews were in the New World as early as the late 1600s. Some newer religions, like Mormonism, were even founded here. In fact, the right to practice your religion freely and without fear is so fundamental in American society that it was guaranteed by the very first amendment made to the Constitution.

One fortunate offshoot of this important principle is the variety of religious architecture in America. From temples and mosques to missions and meetinghouses, religious buildings have always been a special part of the landscape. Generally, these buildings call upon the rituals and symbolism of the religion they house. Cruciform (cross-shaped) floor plans and domes (which represent heaven) are common to cathedrals, for instance, while mosques always face in the direction of Mecca, the Islamic holy city.

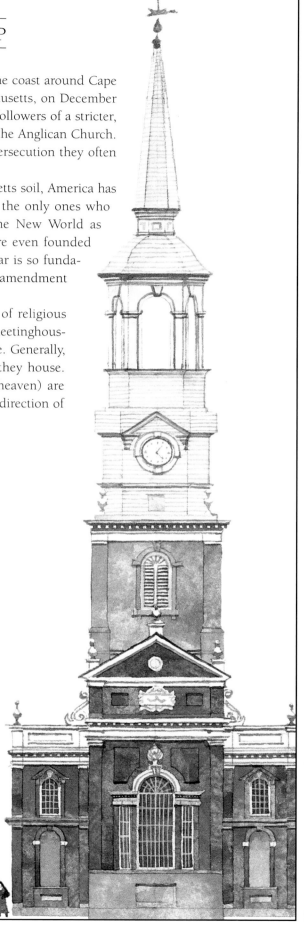

◀ With its twin minarets (towers) and its arched doorways, the **Plum Street Temple** (Cincinnati, Ohio, 1863–65) mimics the Moorish architecture of Spain and North Africa. It also features thirteen Byzantine-style domes (visible only from the inside) and a triple facade and rose window that are typical of Gothic cathedrals. The synagogue's architect, James Keys Wilson, hoped that by mixing these various elements, he would evoke the many different cultures that have influenced Judaism over the centuries.

▶ **Christ Church** (Philadelphia, 1727–44), an Anglican church built in the Georgian style, was the most elaborate and important place of worship in colonial America. Its congregation once included such significant figures as George Washington, Benjamin Franklin, and Betsy Ross. The prominent steeple (completed in 1754) rises up 180 feet, making the church at one time the tallest structure in North America.

◀ For his Roman Catholic **Baltimore Cathedral** (Baltimore, 1804–21), the first cathedral built in the United States, Benjamin Latrobe designed a Latin cross with a massive dome at the point of intersection. Unusually, the circularity of the dome is carried down to the walls below. The neoclassical feel of the cathedral is reinforced in the front portico, which boasts a large triangular pediment and a double row of columns.

One of the very first things the original New England settlers did was establish a place of higher learning. Harvard College, founded in 1636, was the first university in America. In a nation based so heavily on its citizens' right to pursue the religion of their choice, it was only natural that a high value was also placed on education. All of the first universities, Harvard among them, were founded by religious groups and designed primarily for the education of church leaders.

It wasn't until people started to push west that universities and colleges began to broaden their programs. The demand was less for religious instruction and more for practical subjects like agriculture and professions like law and medicine. The College of William and Mary, the second-oldest university in the United States, established the first law school in the country in 1779, and other schools soon followed its lead. When Thomas Jefferson founded the University of Virginia, one of the first state universities, in 1819, he favored a liberal program of study that included courses in arts and sciences, engineering, and of course,

architecture. He even designed the campus to reflect the objectives of the school.

Eventually, this idea that education should be practical and widely available trickled down to elementary and secondary schools as well. High schools were an American invention, and the first one opened in Boston in 1824. Hundreds more soon followed, and many were required by law to teach certain subjects depending on the size of the towns they served: the bigger the town, the more extensive the curriculum.

▼ The **University of Virginia** (Charlottesville, 1823–27) was the first American campus to be built according to a strict design plan. Jefferson was both the university's founder and its architect, and he built the main Rotunda (modeled after the Pantheon in Rome) to house the library. Knowledge, not religion, was to be the focus of this university. Two rows of smaller, pavilion-like buildings flank the Rotunda. Professors lived and taught in these buildings, each of which displays a different order of Roman architecture.

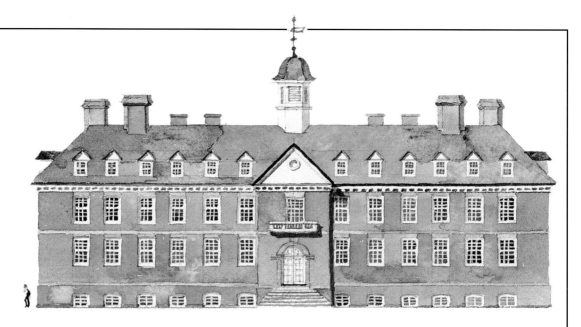

▲ The **College of William and Mary** (Williamsburg, Virginia, 1695–1702) is sometimes called the Wren Building because it is believed to have been based on a design by the famous English architect Sir Christopher Wren. Like many of Wren's buildings, this one has a central cupola, symmetrical windows, and a triangular pediment over the main door.

▲ It seems hard to believe, but **Last Chance Gulch** (now Helena, Montana) was actually quite a sophisticated frontier town. These late 1870s streets might look rugged and crude to a twenty-first-century eye, but the brick buildings indicate a level of elegance few similar towns enjoyed. These buildings even boast arched windows and, in some cases, columns. After a series of fires in the early 1870s destroyed many of the town's original log structures, local residents decided to build again with more durable brick. This lent the town a feeling of permanence – which might be one reason why it grew into what is today a sizable city while so many other gold-rush towns simply disappeared.

▶ For many western migrants, their first frontier home was a **sod house.** These were constructed by laying strips of sod (grass) in rows like bricks. Although they were quick and easy to construct and made effective use of available materials, the settlers detested them and couldn't wait to build something more comfortable and familiar.

GOING WEST

On a sunny January afternoon in 1848, in a creek in northern California, James Marshall bent down and picked up a tiny glittering object that had caught his eye. It was gold, and the California gold rush was on.

The gold rush brought people flooding into California, which wasn't yet a state, in unbelievable numbers. From 1848 to 1850, the population leaped from fewer than 20,000 to more than 100,000. And that was only the beginning. By 1860, almost 400,000 people lived there. Later rushes brought similar numbers to Colorado, Montana, Nevada, and Idaho.

The quest for gold, land, and freedom had once drawn people to the original colonies, and now it was leading them to push beyond the limits of settled territory. Long and dangerous wagon trails were the only way to make the journey west, and one of the most famous of these was the Mormon Trail. The great Mormon leader Brigham Young led his followers along this trail to the Great Salt Lake, in Utah, where he believed they would be able to live free from the intolerance and persecution that had plagued their earlier settlements in Missouri and Illinois.

These trails were only for those with strong wills, however. Not only were they many hundreds of miles long, but they were vulnerable to floods, grass fires, and attacks by hostile Native groups. It took the Mormons, like all other western migrants, months to reach their destination – with few safe places to stop along the way and very little awaiting them once they arrived.

▼ **Fort Laramie** (Laramie, Wyoming, 1834) began life as a trading post. Groups of Natives would bring highly prized buffalo robes to be traded for dry goods, tobacco, and alcohol. Later the fort grew into a waystation for exhausted travelers bound for the rich farmland of Oregon, the Mormon community in Utah, or the goldfields of California. They could buy provisions (flour, dried meat, clothing), repair damaged wagons, or simply enjoy some well-earned rest. It is estimated that at the fort's peak of activity, in 1852, more than 50,000 pioneers passed through on their way to a new life.

▼ Because the railroad began in the east and ended in the west, it seems only fitting that Los Angeles' **Union Station** (Los Angeles, 1936–39) was the last majestic train terminal built in America. The station pays tribute to both its time period and its geographic location by mixing elements of Art Deco and Spanish Mission architecture. The walls, though concrete, suggest the traditional adobe building blocks of the Southwest. Decorative Mexican-style tiles and Art Deco lamps and signs add to the building's unique flavor.

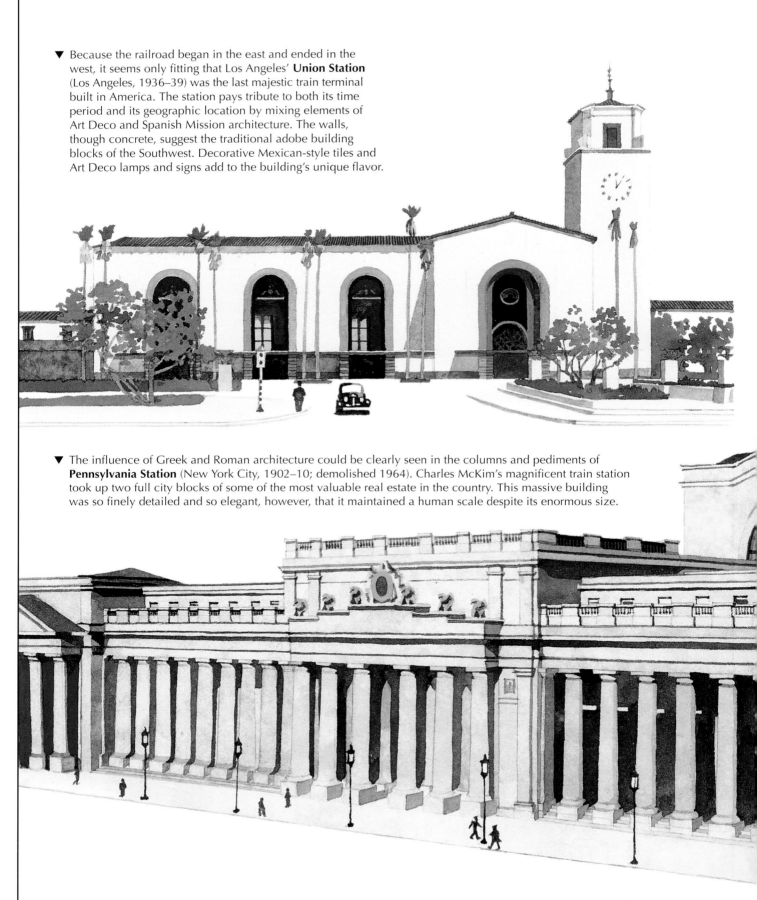

▼ The influence of Greek and Roman architecture could be clearly seen in the columns and pediments of **Pennsylvania Station** (New York City, 1902–10; demolished 1964). Charles McKim's magnificent train station took up two full city blocks of some of the most valuable real estate in the country. This massive building was so finely detailed and so elegant, however, that it maintained a human scale despite its enormous size.

A RIBBON OF STEEL

For more than a quarter of a century, Americans had dreamed of building a railroad that would stretch from the Atlantic to the Pacific, uniting the large, bustling cities of the East with all the promise of the untamed American West. But it wasn't going to be easy. The proposed route, from Sacramento, California, to Omaha, Nebraska (the existing end of the line), traveled through almost 1,800 miles of unforgiving territory. If it was to be completed, railroad workers would have to tunnel through mountains, bridge steep canyons, and keep a watchful eye out for avalanches and hostile Natives. The best plan of attack, it was decided, would be to split the work between two railroad companies: the Central Pacific would start in California and build east while the Union Pacific would start in Nebraska and build west.

The construction proved to be every bit as difficult as people had feared. The Union Pacific in particular ran into problems with shoddy workmanship and eventually a financial scandal that almost ruined the company. But in the end it was all worth it. On May 10, 1869, seven years after Congress had first approved the plan, the dream of a transcontinental railroad came true. In the town of Promontory, Utah, the two separate rail lines met and were joined together with a symbolic gold spike. In short order, more rail lines were completed between Illinois and California, Minnesota and Oregon, and California and Louisiana. There had been only 30,000 miles of track before that amazing day in 1869; by 1900, almost 200,000 miles had been built.

Such a historic accomplishment deserved to be honored in some equally historic architecture. Perhaps the finest railroad terminal on a grand scale was New York's Pennsylvania Station, designed by the famous architecture firm of McKim, Mead and White. By the time the final monumental station was completed – in Los Angeles in 1939 – the golden age of rail travel was all but over.

◀ Thanks to countless movies and television shows like "Little House on the Prairie," the **log house** has entered the popular imagination. In reality, such houses weren't often found on the prairie. Trees were too scarce to be turned into building materials, and when lumber was eventually brought in by train, settlers used it to build frame houses instead. Log houses were popular on the frontier, however, in states like California and Washington, where trees were plentiful and free for the taking.

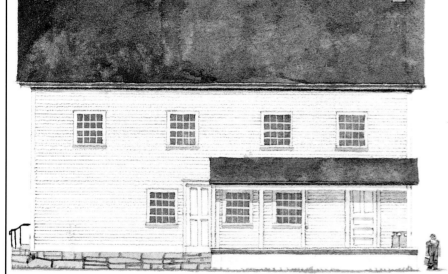

◀ The Shakers ran some of the most successful self-sufficient farming communities between the 1820s and 1860s, though they never ventured farther west than Indiana and Kentucky. This **dairy and weave shop** is a typical Shaker design. It's a wood frame building with clapboards and an uncomplicated gable roof. The simple lines and perfect proportions of their buildings are just two of the reasons Shaker architecture is still so admired (and copied) today.

IN THE HEARTLAND

When the railroad finally came, it changed the nation forever. In the middle of the 1800s, the only people who'd been hardy enough to try to migrate west were missionaries, gold seekers, the Mormons, and a few farm families who headed for a fertile valley in Oregon. But everyone skipped right over the middle of the country, which remained an unexplored wilderness until into the 1870s.

The railroad made the journey west much quicker and less dangerous, and that and an ever-increasing need for land opened up the middle of the country to settlement. But there was a reason why this region had once been considered unlivable: it was a vast plain, with no water to irrigate crops and few trees to cut down for lumber. It was so unappealing, in fact, that it had long been called the Great American Desert.

Starting in the 1860s, with the Homestead Act, Congress began passing laws that made this prairie land cheap and easy to buy. Eventually, the proceeds of these land sales went to fund massive dam projects that would make the soil at least slightly more useful for crops. Technological advancements also allowed farmers to work the land more efficiently. And so-called dry farming techniques, perfect for crops like wheat and corn, turned out to work well in the dry, flat plains.

This once great desert became the breadbasket of the nation, a place of prosperity and promise. When the railroad started bringing back lumber from the thick forests of California and Washington, settlers abandoned their first frontier-style dwellings for more substantial frame houses. The Midwest was booming, and it was time for the temporary settlers to make their lives there more permanent.

▼ The **frame house** was the ultimate goal of the prairie settlers. These simple, unornamented homes were sometimes prefabricated and shipped in pieces from the East. In other cases, they were built from designs found in pattern books that became popular in the mid-nineteenth century.

◀ The White City–inspired classical revival was not the only one taking place in America. Henry Trost's **Second Owls Club** (Tucson, Arizona, 1903) was part of a Spanish Mission revival in the Southwest. Its adobe walls and exposed rafter ends remind us of buildings like Santa Fe's Palace of the Governors (see page 9).

◀ William Le Baron Jenney had built the **Home Insurance Building** (Chicago, 1883–85; demolished 1931) a decade before he designed the Horticulture Building for the Chicago exposition. This is commonly described as the first true skyscraper. It had a frame constructed entirely of iron and steel, instead of brick or stone. The lighter frame meant the masonry foundation could support more floors. An exterior curtain wall of brick and terra cotta dressed up the finished building.

▶ To speed things along, organizers decided that all the buildings in the Chicago exposition's model city – like Richard Morris Hunt's **Administration Building** – would be painted in the same shade of white. They were all constructed of iron, wood, glass, and a new product called staff (Plaster of Paris molded over cloth). Although staff was inexpensive and easy to work with, and could be made to look like marble, stone, rock, or other types of masonry, it was only half an inch thick. It didn't have the durability of stone, which made the buildings vulnerable to the fires that inevitably came.

THE WHITE CITY

Everyone agreed that the only way to mark the 400th anniversary of Christopher Columbus's voyage to America was to mount a massive world's fair. Washington, New York, and St. Louis all competed for the honor of hosting it, but ultimately Chicago was chosen.

The World's Columbian Exposition actually happened one year late, in 1893, but nobody seemed to mind. More than 27 million people attended, and each visitor had the opportunity to experience new products like Juicy Fruit gum and Cracker Jack candy; unfamiliar cultures through exhibits like the Turkish Village, the Street in Cairo, and the Moorish Palace; and technological innovations like the first elevated rail line and the Ferris wheel (one of the most popular attractions).

But the fair's greatest influence was on the architecture of the period. It was decided that all the buildings in the White City, an ideal model metropolis that was the centerpiece of the exposition, should be classical in style. Once again, domes, columns, arches, and porticos were everywhere, calling to mind ancient Greece or Rome. Today this style is most commonly called Beaux Arts because many of the architects who favored it were trained at the École des Beaux-Arts in Paris. It would prove to be the most popular style of architecture in America for the next thirty years.

Unfortunately, the buildings of the White City wouldn't endure quite as well. Although they were never meant to be permanent, they didn't survive as long as intended. A series of fires, culminating in a terrible inferno on July 5, 1894, destroyed most of the fair's significant structures, including all of the White City except for Charles Atwood's Fine Arts Building.

A NEW CENTURY

Louis Sullivan, arguably one of America's greatest architects, once predicted that "the damage wrought by the world's fair will last for half a century from its date, if not longer." In his mind, the classical revival was a huge step backward for architecture – and for the nation.

Sullivan promoted instead the idea of architecture on a human scale, without the unnecessary extravagance of classical detailing. He believed that whatever a building is used for should determine how it looks – that form should follow function, as he liked to say. For his commercial towers, like the Wainright Building in St. Louis, he employed a three-part design, with the bottom floors given over to lobbies and shops, the middle floors to offices, and the top floors to mechanical systems. The different activities taking place on the interiors of his buildings were always clearly expressed in the exterior design.

Many other architects at the start of the new century believed in the same ideas as Sullivan. There was even a movement, called the Chicago School, that fought hard to put these ideas into practice. Architects of the Chicago School included Sullivan, William Le Baron Jenney, and Frank Lloyd Wright.

Wright was Sullivan's most famous student, and he was profoundly influenced by Sullivan's beliefs. He felt that all buildings should be built on a human scale, as Sullivan said, in a style appropriate to their time and place. It was a theory he liked to call organic architecture, and it became one of the most important architectural principles of the twentieth century.

◄ We can see Louis Sullivan's theory of three-part design even in a massive skyscraper like the **Woolworth Building** (New York City, 1911–13). The building starts with a U-shaped base, transforms into a graceful tower, and ends in a copper pinnacle. Designed by Cass Gilbert, it was by far the world's tallest building when it first went up, although today it is dwarfed by its neighbors. The building is remarkably elegant, with finials and crockets that remind us of Gothic churches of old and earned it the nickname the Cathedral of Commerce.

▶ Although the **National Farmers' Bank** (Owatanna, Minnesota, 1907–08) is small in scale, it still demonstrates the three-part design Louis Sullivan also used for his skyscrapers. Here the base is simple red sandstone and the cap a protruding cornice. But the focal point is the building's midsection, a beautiful band of green terra cotta framing a semicircular mosaic window and punctuated by decorative brown terra cotta carvings. The amount of detailing, while beautiful, is evidence that Sullivan didn't always follow his own theories.

▲ For the **Larkin Building** (Buffalo, New York, 1903–04; demolished 1950), Frank Lloyd Wright designed an enclosed courtyard with galleries of office space surrounding it. Like today's modern office buildings, it was air-conditioned and completely sealed off from the outside world (to protect employees from the soot and grime of its industrial setting). Wright hoped that a building directed in toward its center, instead of out toward the street, would create a community feeling among the Larkin employees.

FRANK LLOYD WRIGHT'S PRAIRIE STYLE

In the early part of the new century, there emerged from the heartland of America – midwestern states like Illinois, Iowa, and Wisconsin – and the office of the great architect Frank Lloyd Wright a new theory of design that came to be called the Prairie School. Wright's belief, and the basis of this theory, was that buildings should exist in harmony with nature, and that they should seem almost to grow from the landscape around them. In the flat, treeless prairies of the Midwest, this meant low, horizontal buildings that seemed to stretch out instead of up.

Wright put his ideas into practice with a series of Prairie Style houses in the early 1900s. These were long, low houses that were always built of what Wright called organic materials – brick, wood, and concrete, mostly – and these materials were left in their natural state, undisguised by paint or plaster. On the inside, Wright got rid of any unnecessary walls so the rooms would flow into each other, and he always made the fireplace the focal point.

With the exception of the windows, which he filled with decorative stained glass designed specially for each client, Wright preferred a look that was streamlined, solid, and uncomplicated by a lot of detailing. This preference was shared by the other architects of the Prairie School, including Irving Gill and the husband-and-wife team of Walter Burley Griffin and Marion Mahony. "We should build our houses simple, plain and substantial as a boulder," Gill once explained, "then leave the ornamentation of it to Nature, who will tone it with lichens, chisel it with storms, make it gracious and friendly with vines and flower shadows as she does the stone in the meadow."

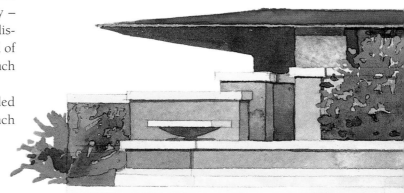

▼ It is easy to see Wright's ideas at work in the designs of his student Marion Mahony. Her **Adolph Mueller House** (Decatur, Illinois, 1910) has the low hipped roofs of the Robie House, as well as the horizontal bands between the first and second stories, and between the first story and the foundation. The slightly upturned eaves might suggest a Japanese pagoda, and the leaded-glass windows are an Arts and Crafts detail.

▼ In **Robie House** (Chicago, Illinois, 1908–09), Wright's Prairie Style masterpiece, we can see the influence of both Japanese design (in the open-concept interiors, the horizontal lines, and the low-pitched roofs with large overhangs) and the English Arts and Crafts movement (in the centrally located hearth, the large porches that seem to invite the outside in, and the decorative window glass and wood detailing that warm the interior), but he really created something unique. Many of his theories about space planning and design are still used today. In fact, Robie House is widely considered one of the most significant buildings in the history of residential architecture.

▼ Sometimes called the Robie House of the West, Irving Gill's **Walter Dodge House** (Los Angeles, 1916; demolished 1970) was like a bridge between several architectural eras. In its smooth walls and rounded arched doorways was the influence of the Mission style. Its low, horizontal lines owed a debt to the Prairie School. And the simplicity of the design and Gill's choice of reinforced concrete for the building material anticipated the International Style architects of the 1960s and 1970s.

▲ The Greene brothers' **Gamble House** (Pasadena, California, 1907–08) is widely considered to be the masterwork of the Arts and Crafts movement. The house is clad in cedar shakes, like the Shingle Style homes of the East Coast, and it shows the influences of other cultures as well. The large overhangs, exposed rafter ends, and visible structural timbers, for example, are clearly inspired by Japanese design. Like Wright, Greene and Greene felt that the architect's responsibility didn't stop with the building itself. For the Gamble House, they also designed all of the furniture, the light fixtures, some of the rugs, and even the door handles and switchplates.

ARTS AND CRAFTS

The Industrial Revolution brought many positive changes to the Western world: increased productivity, more wealth, and a better overall standard of living, to name just a few. But not everyone believed all the changes were for the better. In England, the poet and designer William Morris spearheaded the Arts and Crafts movement, a reaction to the mass production of goods made possible by new technologies and increased mechanization. Morris wanted people to take a renewed interest in unique, handcrafted design. He believed, as he once said, in art "for the people by the people."

Morris's ideas found a receptive audience in America, especially among furniture designers like Gustav Stickley and architects like Frank Lloyd Wright. But the American Arts and Crafts movement is most closely associated with California and the work of architects like Greene and Greene (the brothers Henry and Charles Sumner Greene) and Bernard Maybeck.

At its heart, the Arts and Crafts movement was highly democratic, which is one reason why it flourished in the United States. One of its key principles was that handmade objects – from furniture to textiles to entire homes – should be affordable and available to everyone. Like Morris, Maybeck and the Greene brothers felt that beautiful things should not be limited to the wealthy. Maybeck even said that he designed for the man in the street, "for he's the one who'll buy the building after the owner sells it."

The Arts and Crafts architects also believed in "honest" design. They liked to leave beams and joints exposed so that anyone who looked at their buildings would be able to see exactly how they were put together. For the most part, they also preferred to work with organic materials, like wood and stone, and to leave these materials in their natural state. These three things – an appreciation of nature, a love of fine craftsmanship, and a belief in honest design – are what the Arts and Crafts movement was all about.

▼ Many different influences are visible in Bernard Maybeck's masterful **First Church of Christ, Scientist** (Berkeley, California, 1910–12). The low, horizontal lines of the building remind us of Frank Lloyd Wright's Prairie houses. The ceremonial entryway has the flavor of Japanese design. Ornamental window tracery calls to mind the Gothic cathedrals of the twelfth and thirteenth centuries. And the exposed asbestos sheathing is an innovative use of modern materials that anticipates late-twentieth-century design. That Maybeck was able to bring together so many dissimilar styles and create such an unusual building is testament to his genius as an architect.

▲ It may be most famous as the spot where the stars leave their hand- and footprints in cement, but **Graumann's Chinese Theatre** (Los Angeles, 1927) is also a dramatic Art Deco treasure. Designed to resemble a Chinese temple, the theater features a copper-clad pagoda roof that sits on two massive wooden pillars shooting copper flames. A closer look reveals tiny stylized dragons that seem to dance along the flames and up and down the roofline.

◄ As well as being the most recognizable example of Art Deco architecture, the **Chrysler Building** (New York City, 1928–30) is a monument to America's love affair with the automobile. Gargoyles shaped like eagle-head hood ornaments project from the fifty-ninth floor, and ornamental brickwork designed to look like car tires and bumpers decorates the facade farther down. But the building is most famous for its tower, a series of gleaming stainless-steel arches that are punctuated by triangular windows and climb toward the building's spire.

THE JAZZ AGE

At the eleventh hour of the eleventh day of the eleventh month, in the year 1918, the Armistice was signed, bringing an end to the First World War and ushering in a period of peace and unprecedented prosperity in the United States. People made fortunes on the stock exchange, and a consumer revolution brought cars, telephones, and countless other modern conveniences to the masses. Life became freer, faster, and more optimistic. This was the Jazz Age – a time of flappers and speakeasies, bathtub gin and the charleston – and its unofficial spokesperson was the writer F. Scott Fitzgerald, the epitome of 1920s excess.

In architecture and the decorative arts (such as furniture, jewelry, and interior design), this became known as the Art Deco period (after the 1925 Exposition of Decorative Arts in Paris). To capture the exuberance of the age, designers began experimenting with dynamic colors like reds, greens, and golds and bold geometric shapes like triangles, curves, chevrons, and zigzags. They also turned for inspiration to what were to them exotic cultures, especially Egypt, China, and the ancient Mayan civilizations of Central America. And they rejected the handmade detailing of the Arts and Crafts movement, making use of design elements from machine-made products like cars, ships, and airplanes instead. Art Deco was a carefree, extravagant style that allowed America to show off its newfound confidence to the world.

▼ Miami boasts the best-preserved Art Deco district in the country, and its small hotels, like the **Carlyle** (Miami, 1941), are especially legendary. Here, though, the bold reds and greens of traditional Art Deco have been replaced by pastel blues, yellows, and pinks that are more in keeping with the seaside setting. Throughout the district, pink flamingos and tropical plants and flowers provide the decoration, while rounded corners and porthole windows conjure up the steamships that once anchored just offshore.

HOMES OF GRANDEUR

The publishing tycoon William Randolph Hearst wrote to his architect, Julia Morgan, in 1919 with a simple request: "Miss Morgan, we are tired of camping out in the open at the ranch in San Simeon and I would like to build a little something." That "little something" turned out to be a massive estate in the style of a medieval hilltop castle. It was built over two decades, and the construction probably would have gone on longer had Hearst not eventually run out of money.

In building San Simeon, Hearst joined the long line of successful American captains of industry who have commissioned for themselves unique and majestic private homes. In a nation that likes to celebrate individual achievement, wealth, and power, these homes were a very public way to display success and accomplishment. And because money was never an object, they were also an opportunity for their architects to try out some of their boldest, most unusual ideas. Built with the best materials over a period of many years, these homes are now some of America's most distinctive architectural treasures.

▼ There is no better example of Frank Lloyd Wright's theory that buildings should grow out from their sites than **Fallingwater** (Mill Run, Pennsylvania, 1935–37). Built as a summer house for Edgar Kaufmann, the owner of a Pittsburgh department store, Fallingwater is anchored to stone cliffs and hangs (precariously, it seems) right over a waterfall. It is such a part of the landscape that some of the larger boulders of the cliffside actually intrude into the house itself and form a section of the living-room floor.

▶ Ordinarily, a French château would seem out of place in the eastern United States, but this massive stone mansion fits well within its mountainous surroundings. Built by Richard Morris Hunt for George W. Vanderbilt, **Biltmore** (Asheville, North Carolina, 1890–95) once sat on 120,000 acres of property designed by the famous landscape architect Frederick Law Olmstead. With its 250 rooms and its four acres of floor space, Biltmore is the largest private home ever built in America.

◀ Also called Hearst Castle, **San Simeon** (San Simeon, California, 1919–39) is actually a complex of several buildings, the largest of which, Casa Grande, amounts to more than 60,000 square feet of space. Although the estate was built using modern materials, it mixes Renaissance and Gothic elements. The towers that flank the main entrance are modeled after some that William Randolph Hearst admired on a church in Ronda, in southern Spain.

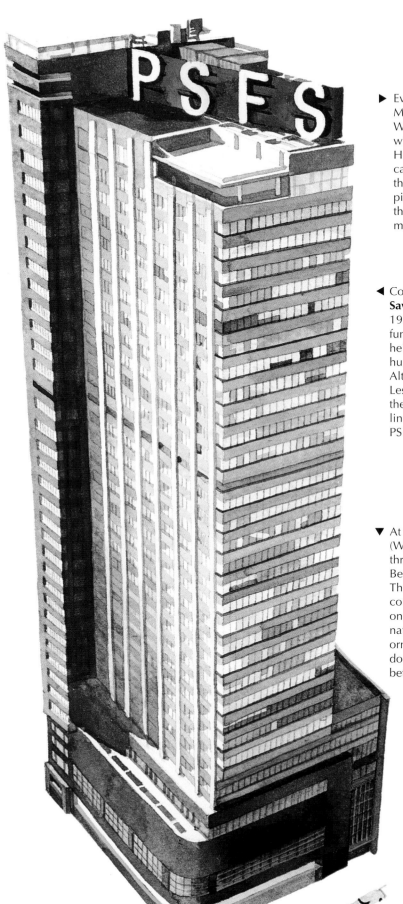

▶ Even Frank Lloyd Wright tried his hand at Streamline Moderne. The **Johnson Wax Building** (Racine, Wisconsin, 1936–39) once again shows his fascination with unconventional building materials and techniques. Here he designed massive concrete pillars, sometimes called lily pads, to support the roof and add drama to the great workroom. Although they look delicate, the pillars are capable of supporting six times the weight they need to. What appear to be skylights are actually milky glass light tubes that simulate daylight.

◀ Considered the first modern skyscraper, the **Philadelphia Savings Fund Society (PSFS) Building** (Philadelphia, 1929–32) is a perfect example of the stripped-down functionality of Streamline Moderne. The building's height is offset by the strong horizontal banding and the hundreds of windows, which wrap around the corners. Although the architects, George Howe and William Lescaze, used a variety of materials for different parts of the building, they still managed to maintain that stream-lined look. The most flashy thing on it is the massive PSFS sign, now a Philadelphia landmark.

▼ At first glance, the marble-covered **National Gallery** (Washington, D.C., 1938–41) seems like a complete throwback to the neoclassicism of buildings like Benjamin Latrobe's Bank of Pennsylvania (see page 13). The architect, John Russell Pope, chose this imposing, conservative style because he thought it was the only one appropriate for a building that was to hold the nation's art collection. But the gallery is less fussy and ornamented than most neoclassical buildings, and it does have the sleek, clean lines that were popular between the wars.

THE DIRTY THIRTIES

It was perhaps inevitable that the free-spending optimism of the 1920s would not last. All over the country, people were overextending themselves – buying on credit, speculating in the stock market, living beyond their means. As the 1920s drew to a close, the inevitable did happen: on October 29, 1929, the stock market crashed, sending America hurtling into the Great Depression.

The Depression was a time of unrelenting misery. At its height, almost 16 million Americans were out of work, and many millions more were dependent on relief agencies for some level of support and assistance. Predictably, people began to reconsider the excesses and extravagance of the 1920s, turning back to values and traditions that had seemed old-fashioned not so long before.

In architecture, there was once again a return to classicism. All those pediments and columns seemed to evoke a solidity and dependability that was needed in this time of turmoil. But there were still people who didn't want to fully abandon the unique design work of the Jazz Age. These architects developed a new style, often called Streamline Moderne, that stripped away the flashy ornamentation of Art Deco and focused instead on clean, simplified lines, functionality, and pragmatic materials like plastic and chrome. This was the beginning of what we now call Modernism.

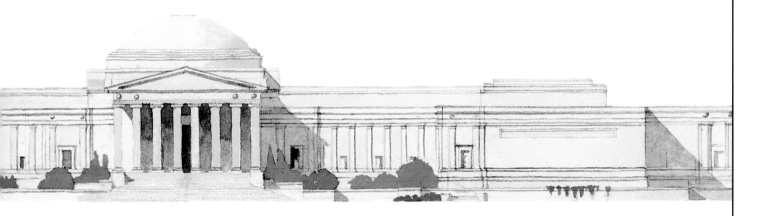

▼ The **ranch house**, with its prominently placed garage, is one of the most instantly recognizable symbols of American suburban life. To keep costs down, most builders kept detailing to a minimum, but the long, low lines and overhanging roof of the typical ranch house do owe something to Frank Lloyd Wright and his Prairie Style of the 1910s.

SUBURBAN LIVING

Having survived poverty and want in the 1930s and a worldwide war in the 1940s, Americans were ready to embrace life again in the 1950s. A new confidence in the future sparked a baby boom and levels of consumer spending that hadn't been seen in decades. People wanted to start families and put down roots – they wanted to buy houses.

Throughout the Depression and the Second World War, very little home building had gone on in the United States. In the 1930s, no one had had the money to buy, and then everyone's attention was focused on the war effort. But generous loan programs for returning soldiers fueled an explosion in the housing market in the late 1940s. Soon there were more new homes being built than at any time since the 1920s.

Of course, there wasn't really room for all these new houses in the already overcrowded downtowns of most of America's major cities. But massive highway-building projects and the spread of the automobile made it possible for more and more people to move into the suburbs, where land was cheaper and more plentiful. When home builders discovered the possibilities of mass production, with preassembled components being shipped to building sites and turned into dozens of identical houses, the final piece of the puzzle fell into place. The dream of home ownership became an affordable reality for millions.

▲ Suburban life would not have been possible without that favorite American modern convenience, the car. Areas that had once been farmland were soon taken up by gas stations and prominent signage that would be clearly visible to people zipping by in cars instead of strolling past on foot.

▼ The first real **planned suburb** was Levittown, Long Island, founded in 1947 by the builder William Levitt. In no time, the country was dotted with similar neighborhoods: block after block of identical houses, all set back on large lots with very few mature trees. It would be some time before these planned communities began to take on a character of their own.

THE INTERNATIONAL STYLE

By the 1950s, the world really had become a global village. Better communications technologies and advancements in air travel made it easy for people to learn about and visit other parts of the globe. And it was easier for ideas to travel as well.

In 1919, a German architect named Walter Gropius had founded a design school he called the Bauhaus. Gropius had a fondness for technology and a dislike of tradition, and he brought these ideas with him when he immigrated to America in 1939. His arrival – and the arrival six years earlier of another Bauhaus director, Ludwig Mies van der Rohe – signaled the start of an architectural revolution in America that came to be called the International Style.

Mies once simply defined his theory of design as "less is more," and this could be called the rallying cry of the International Style architects. Gropius, Mies, and others like them favored machine-made design over handcrafting and innovation over tradition. They also preferred distinctly modern materials, such as steel, glass, and concrete, and strong, crisp geometric lines.

Put simply, the International Style architects wanted to strip their buildings down to their bare essentials, leaving them uncluttered by ornamentation or decorative accents, and make a total break with the past. They believed that by creating buildings that looked the same in Houston, Texas, and Harare, Zimbabwe, they would rid them of associations with specific cultures or environments and free them to be whatever they wanted to be.

◀ A masterpiece of modern design, Ludwig Mies van der Rohe's box-like **Seagram Building** (New York City, 1954–58) is deceptively simple. Row upon row of elegant bronze floor-to-ceiling windows climb above New York's exclusive Park Avenue, while an expansive granite forecourt with twin reflecting pools sets the building back from the street. The Seagram Building has the streamlined appearance and lack of detailing we expect of a Modernist structure, but it still manages to look rich and ornate because of the materials used.

▼ The seventeen triangular spires of the **Air Force Academy Chapel** (Colorado Springs, Colorado, 1956–62) resemble both airplane wings and hands brought together in prayer. Although it seems to be a very non-traditional religious building, the chapel does make extensive use of stained glass, while the triangles are a modernized take on Gothic church steeples. The building is a little unusual for the firm of Skidmore, Owings and Merrill because it does have a more obvious nod to the past than we usually associate with International Style architects.

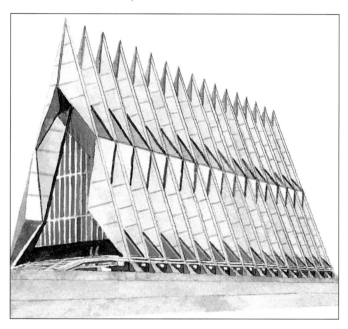

▼ The Modernists' love of stripped-down, unornamented design is taken to an extreme in Philip Johnson's **Glass House** (New Canaan, Connecticut, 1949), which is, as its name suggests, a house constructed almost entirely of glass. A large brick cylinder in the middle of the building helps divide the space, as well as hiding the bathroom from prying eyes. The rest of the home is fully exposed to the great outdoors.

▼ Walter Gropius's **Pan Am Building** (New York City, 1959–63), now called the MetLife Building, was hated when it was first built because it so dwarfed its Park Avenue neighbors. Once the world's largest office tower in bulk, the Pan Am Building is less overpowering than it might have been, thanks to its octagonal design and the horizontal banding of the two mechanical floors, which house the building's heating and air-conditioning systems and help break the monotony of the facade.

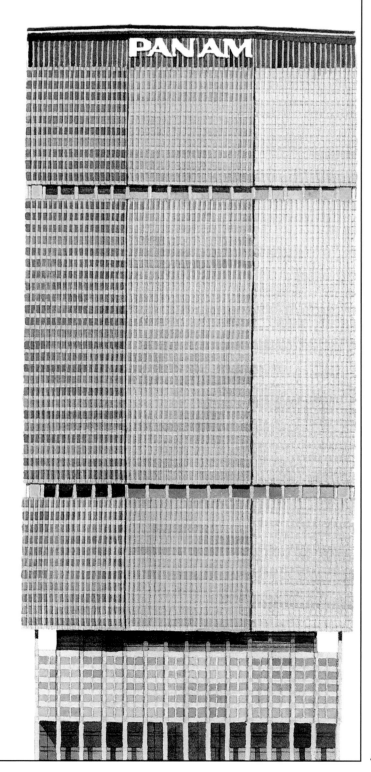

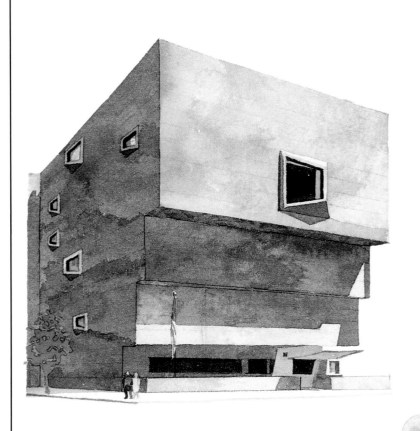

▶ When he was designing the **Richards Medical Research Building** (Philadelphia, 1957–61), Louis Kahn started by organizing it into what he called "servant" and "served" spaces. The served spaces – the offices and research labs – are contained in a series of glass towers. Attached to these are taller brick-clad towers that hold the servant spaces – the animal quarters, mechanical systems, and washrooms. Here the sense of movement is captured in the fluctuations of the facade and the constantly varying heights of the towers.

◀ For the **Whitney Museum of American Art** (New York City, 1964–66), Marcel Breuer wanted to create a building that would hold its own in a neighborhood of towering skyscrapers but still be on a more intimate scale. The bold cantilevers and irregularly shaped windows of the granite building he designed help it stand out in a city full of architectural marvels.

▶ With its gently curved roof, the terminal building at **Dulles International Airport** (Chantilly, Virginia, 1958–62) seems almost ready to take flight. Not only is this sense of movement a key element of later Modernist design, but it is also highly appropriate for a structure dedicated to travel. Eero Saarinen, the architect, called the building "the best thing I have done."

SPACE AGE EXPRESSIONISM

In 1961, John F. Kennedy promised that Americans would land safely on the moon before the decade was out. His prediction, which Neil Armstrong made true in 1969, sparked a space race between the United States and the then Soviet Union that lasted for decades.

There was a boldness in the race to put a man on the moon that could only have come in the 1960s. This was a decade of great change and upheaval, the era of civil rights and the women's movement, hippies and the Vietnam War. It was a period that was to transform America forever – socially, culturally, and of course, architecturally.

Perhaps encouraged by the space race and the vision of the future it represented, or maybe just picking up on the

rebellious spirit of the times, many architects of the middle to late 1960s started designing buildings that were more dynamic and unconventional than those generally seen in the 1950s and early 1960s. They rejected the uniform box-like skyscrapers of Ludwig Mies van der Rohe and the earlier Modernists in favor of smaller-scale structures that were almost sculptural in design, and that had a renewed emphasis on form and function. It was as if the restless feeling that had seized the nation as a whole began to find expression in the architecture of the period as well.

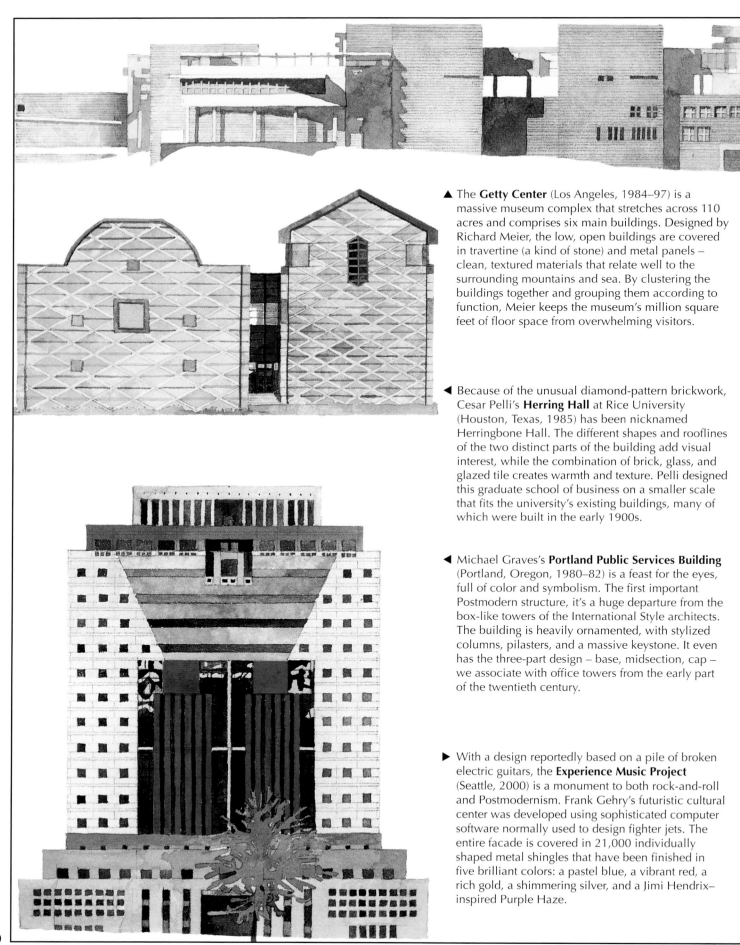

▲ The **Getty Center** (Los Angeles, 1984–97) is a massive museum complex that stretches across 110 acres and comprises six main buildings. Designed by Richard Meier, the low, open buildings are covered in travertine (a kind of stone) and metal panels – clean, textured materials that relate well to the surrounding mountains and sea. By clustering the buildings together and grouping them according to function, Meier keeps the museum's million square feet of floor space from overwhelming visitors.

◄ Because of the unusual diamond-pattern brickwork, Cesar Pelli's **Herring Hall** at Rice University (Houston, Texas, 1985) has been nicknamed Herringbone Hall. The different shapes and rooflines of the two distinct parts of the building add visual interest, while the combination of brick, glass, and glazed tile creates warmth and texture. Pelli designed this graduate school of business on a smaller scale that fits the university's existing buildings, many of which were built in the early 1900s.

◄ Michael Graves's **Portland Public Services Building** (Portland, Oregon, 1980–82) is a feast for the eyes, full of color and symbolism. The first important Postmodern structure, it's a huge departure from the box-like towers of the International Style architects. The building is heavily ornamented, with stylized columns, pilasters, and a massive keystone. It even has the three-part design – base, midsection, cap – we associate with office towers from the early part of the twentieth century.

▶ With a design reportedly based on a pile of broken electric guitars, the **Experience Music Project** (Seattle, 2000) is a monument to both rock-and-roll and Postmodernism. Frank Gehry's futuristic cultural center was developed using sophisticated computer software normally used to design fighter jets. The entire facade is covered in 21,000 individually shaped metal shingles that have been finished in five brilliant colors: a pastel blue, a vibrant red, a rich gold, a shimmering silver, and a Jimi Hendrix–inspired Purple Haze.

POSTMODERNISM

As the country entered the final quarter-century of the millennium, the stark Modernist vision of the International Style architects was put down and a new theory of architecture, Postmodernism, began to take its place.

Postmodernism is all about variety, individualism, and diversity. Some architects of this school have returned to traditional styles, employing design elements and color schemes that were rejected by the Modernists. Gone are the towering, stripped-down, monochromatic skyscrapers of the 1960s and 1970s. These Postmodernists build on a more human scale, with an awareness of and appreciation for surrounding structures and the physical environment. And while they still try to create buildings that are completely of their own time, they often use materials and details that recall earlier eras.

Other Postmodernists, sometimes called Deconstructivists, produce structures that look haphazard and even chaotic. Their buildings follow unexpected lines or jut out suddenly at extreme and aggressive angles. There is the suggestion in them that it is pointless to search for order in what is fundamentally a disordered world. At the opposite end of the scale, New Urbanists promote a return to community-based living, and proponents of "green" building urge us to adopt recycled and environmentally responsible products.

As we move into the new millennium, it is impossible to say which of these styles will endure and which will falter. The real excitement lies in waiting to see what today's architects will think of next.

GLOSSARY

arch

crocket

dormer window

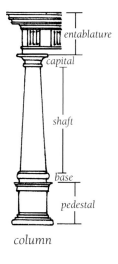

column

finial

ADOBE:
a sun-dried brick of mud or clay and straw

ARCH:
a curved or pointed structure spanning an opening

ASYMMETRY:
in architecture, refers to a structure that is dissimilar in size and
shape on either side of a central line

BAROQUE:
a heavily ornamented style of architecture of the seventeenth and
eighteenth centuries

CANTILEVER:
a projection or overhang that has no obvious bracing or is fixed only at one end

CAST IRON:
iron shaped by being poured into molds

COLUMN:
an upright support or pillar, often designed in one of three styles – Doric,
Ionic, or Corinthian

CORNICE:
a decorative molding that runs along the top of a building or wall

CROCKET:
a small carved ornament, often a leaf, that is affixed to the slope of a spire,
pinnacle, finial, etc.

CRUCIFORM:
shaped like a cross

CUPOLA:
a small rounded dome that tops off a roof

CURTAIN WALL:
an outside wall that is attached to the frame of a building but gives no support

DOME:
a rounded roof, often with a circular base

DORMER WINDOW:
a window projecting from a sloping roof

EAVE:
the underside of a sloping roof, overhanging a wall

FACADE:
the face of a building

FINIAL:
a small ornament at the top of a roof, gable, or other high projection

FRIEZE:
a decorative band that runs along the top of a wall, below the cornice

GABLE:
the triangular portion of a wall at the end of a pitched roof

gable

GALERIE:
a large, French-inspired porch, usually running the length of the
second floor of a house

GARGOYLE:
a projection from a roof, wall, or tower that is carved into a grotesque figure

gargoyle

GOTHIC:
a style of architecture of the twelfth to sixteenth centuries, characterized
by pointed arches, vaults, and flying buttresses

HIPPED ROOF:
a roof that slopes on all four sides

KEYSTONE:
the central stone of an arch

keystone

MASONRY:
stonework or brickwork; any work done by a mason

MINARET:
a tall tower or turret, most often associated with mosques

MORTAR:
a mixture used to adhere bricks or stone together

minaret

MOSAIC:
decoration (artwork, murals) made from small pieces of glass or stone

OVERHANG:
the projecting part of a roof or the upper story of a house

PAGODA:
a Chinese-, Japanese-, or Indian-style temple

PEDIMENT:
a triangular-shaped gable above a portico, door, window, etc.

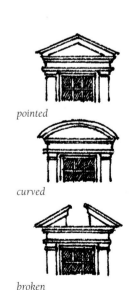
pointed

curved

broken

pediments

PILASTER:
a column projecting only slightly from a wall

PINNACLE:
the small, turret-like end of a spire, buttress, etc.

PITCHED ROOF:
a roof with two sloped sides and gables at both ends

PORTICO:
a structure consisting of a roof supported by columns and topped
by a pediment, usually attached as a porch or entryway to a
building; also called a temple front

pinnacle

portico

PREFABRICATE:
to manufacture whole buildings or their components in a factory prior to transportation to a building site

RAFTER:
a timber or beam that supports a roof

ROTUNDA:
a circular-shaped room, usually domed

SANDSTONE:
a soft, usually pinkish-red sedimentary rock made of grains of sand

SHEATHING:
a layer of plywood or other material covering the framing of a building

SPIRE:
a tall, pointed structure topping a roof, tower, turret, etc.

STEEPLE:
the tower and spire of a church

SYMMETRY:
in architecture, refers to a structure that has parts of equal size and shape on either side of a plane, line, or point

TEMPLE FRONT:
see PORTICO

TERRA COTTA:
unglazed, usually red-brown tile that is used decoratively because it can be modeled or fitted into molds

TRACERY:
a delicate decorative pattern on a window made with stone or wooden bars and mullions; associated with Gothic architecture

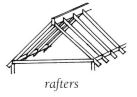

rafters

steeple

tracery

INDEX

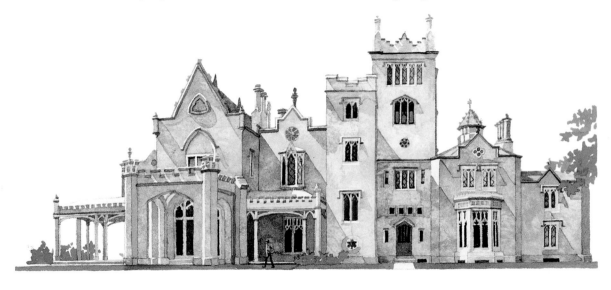